# He Was With Me All The Time

Ahshell R. Brown

ISBN: 0692292225
ISBN-13: 978-0692292228

# DEDICATION

I will like to dedicate this book to God and anyone who have ever suffered from hurt and pain in their life. The kind of pain that has shaped how you think about yourself. The kind of hurt that I'm speaking about, you have lived with for years. There have been moments when you have thought, that just maybe you shouldn't be alive any more. You are not alone no matter how much you may feel like it. There are people out there who have been hurt just like you. You don't have to feel alone because you are not alone.

Father God loves you more than any human being can ever love you. So, remember to always be honest with yourself about your feelings and with others. Never build walls out of hurt but be determined to love hard and trust God in all you do. You can make it in life and your happiness is just one prayer, and one step away. Be true to yourself and shoot for the stars, skies are the limit. No matter what you have faced in life you do not have to be enslaved to the pain that you have experienced, but you can rise above all that tries to hold you down. There is inner strength that you have not even tapped into yet. So, arise and shine for you light have come.

Isaiah 60:1 KJV
Ahshell B

# Prayer

Dear Heavenly Father I give this book back to you and I pray that it will touch the lives of your people. I seek for deliverance to take place after reading this book and I thank you for the favor that you have placed on this book and the anointing you have put in my hands. Touch the mindset of your people and I decree and declare peace and wholeness in their lives. I bind up depression, suicide, and any spirit of darkness that tries to take your people out every day. May your peace Lord and your healing power be seen upon the lives of your people? Help guide your people to think higher and understand you more, and the plan that you have for their lives. You are God and you are God alone through the good times and through the bad. I thank you for the transformation that has taken place in my life. I am thankful for my compassion for your people. Lord please teach us how to love one another the more and live our lives to bring glory to your holy name. Have your way in the life of every person that reads this book. I declare that the chains and bondage of your people are broken and they will walk in the freedom that you have given them.


In Jesus name I prayer,

Amen

# CONTENTS

Introduction

# INTRODUCTION

This is a book that talks about the hurt and pain that I grew up with in my childhood into my adulthood. I wanted to be honest about the things that I felt as I went through different stages in life. My objective is to reach people who are struggling with depression, suicide, loneliness, low self-esteem, and all other hurt and pain that are not healthy to the mind, body, and soul. This book will cause people to see that there is deliverance after the hurt. Our love ones are out there hurting every day and we don't even realize it, or we do realize it but don't take time to help them realize that they can be healed from their hurts. Be honest with yourself and take the walls down. You don't have to walk around in life with walls only letting people in but so far, because you can miss out on good relationships and great experiences. You can't hide behind the anger anymore because your happiness depends on it. How will you ever reach your maximize potential out of life. With those walls and hurts that most people don't know about.

God loves you and he wants the very best for you. You can be a better mother, sister, wife or friend. Embrace yourself and enjoy who you are and all your differences. As you read each chapter keep your own life difficulties in mind and decide to be better and do more. I present to you a book that is filled with my life and the things that I have faced, but to also encourage and lift others up as well. There are three different phase to this book to show the phase that I have went through in life. My motherhood stage is more about maturity and what God can do for you. Where the other two stages deal more with pain and my actions because of my hurt. Even though this book is more for women it doesn't take anyway the fact that people of all genders hurt, as we go through life. So please read and be healed from heartbreak and despair. No matter what stage of life you are in this is just the beginning and your future will be greater than your beginning. Take the time to deal with the issues that no one wants to talk about. I found out that in life most people cover up their hurt and then say that they are healed but God wants all his children to be healed for real.

As I walk you through my life stories I pray that it will cause you to take a look at your life and be honest with yourself. I pray that this book will cause you to face the issues that you have sweep under the rug. Let's take a look at our giants together and dig our heals in the ground, and decide that the past will go no further in our future with us than it has already.

# ACKNOWLEDGEMENTS

I will like to thank God for giving me the vision to write this book, and opening doors that I never thought were possible. It is because of God that I am able to do this. I am thankful for my husband and for my children for always loving me and believing in me. I am also thankful to all those who have prayed me through my struggles with birthing out this book. God has placed some wonderful people in my path and it is because of all of you that I am the person that you see today. Thank You all for believing in me when I didn't believe in myself.

# Adolescence

# Chapter 1 – The Stage of Growing Up

Adolescence is viewed as a transitional period whose chief purpose is the preparation of children for adult roles. These are the years that will shape our children into the young adults that they will become. This stage of life is so very important and we as parents need to understand that so much go on in this stage of life with our children. Their minds and bodies are changing right before their eyes and they have to deal with peer-pressure like never before. It is in this stage that our children transition from child and begin to mature into adult. I was talking to a girlfriend of mine not too long ago and I was telling her about some things in my life. As I began to tell her about the things that I have been through, I realize that I went through an awful lot through my adolescence stage. The more we continue to talk the more I realized that I was in a stage of transition.

How I was at a place in my life where I needed to figure out who I was. Now I can look back and see that I have said and done things in that stage of my life that I am not proud of, but it's because I am sure of myself today that I can reflect in such a manner. This was a place in my life when I needed and wanted to have some kind of an idea of the type of adult that I wanted to become. I needed guidance and strong leadership to teach me about being a good person and instilling good values in me. This was not the point where I needed more negativity, but I needed positivity and love. During this period in my life there was more negativity in my life and I started to allow myself to become a victim to it. I never really had someone to say that I could make it and succeed in life.

# He Was With Me All The Time

As a matter of fact, I never had anyone talk to me about my future at all. I was left to kind of figure it out on my own, and there are children out there today in the same place that I was in. When our children are in that place, you leave to many open doors for things to enter in and influence our children. There were a lot of things I learned from the streets. As parents these are the times where we should pour into our kids. There is more to life than just going to work or church every day, and what is the point of building someone else establishment (your job or someone else's ministry) when you do not pour into your own children. So many times, we look to get a shot at being someone important to other people. We are upset because no one will give us a chance to prove our ministry or allow us to show that we are anointed; but in fact, your ministry is at home. It has already started with your family. Build your family and then you will understand how to build a ministry.

# Chapter 2 - Pain

I was five years old when I moved from Mount Vernon, New York to Detroit Michigan. My sister who is fifteen years older than I asked if I wanted to come and visit Detroit for a summer? Well that summer has lasted over 28 years now. I have small memories of my father when I was in New York but I always remember my mother working as a single parent. She worked long shifts and wasn't the most affectionate person and I wasn't sure that she loved me but now I know she loves me. By me growing up in a single parent home I didn't have that love from a father. My father lived in New York and he had a family besides myself to take care of. He played such a big part in my life even though he wasn't there. I didn't love myself or even like myself and I was desperate for someone to love me. Many choices that I made would have been different if my father was in my life.

 When I was much younger my Mom was an alcoholic and so was my long distinct father. My mother didn't show affection and I didn't have my father to show me love, and I was always called fat. My family is very opinionated and I was always talked down too, after all I was the baby. So, I wasn't allowed to say much. I felt like I was a mistake because my Mom had me in her late thirties, and my father had his own family. I was so desperate to hear the words I love you that I would have probably did just about anything to hear those words spoken to me. I am well off into my adulthood and I have still never heard those three words from my mother. My father told me that he loved me every time that I spoke with him on the phone. But that was followed by a lie or broken promises that he always made to me. Everyone in this world need love no matter how young or old.

# He Was With Me All The Time

So, I began to look for love in all the wrong places. I began acting out and trying to find comfort from my friend's families, hoping that maybe they will accept me as one of their own. Well that didn't quit work out either. So, I use to sit in my room and cry, wondering why God would allow me to be born into a family like this. I had a brother who was eight years older than me and he act as if he hated my guts. He would call me names like ding bat, and my mom would call me tubby. I always felt like God was with me and looking out for me but it was a lot of things that I did not understand. I remember one time my mother, brother, and myself were at home sleep and I woke up in the middle of the night by what I thought was sun rays. Well I got out of bed and notice that the front door was opened so I went to the door only to find everyone standing outside. I go outside and the sun rays that I thought was coming through my window was actually the side of my house on fire. I said mom what happen and she looked at me and said how did you get out here?

By the time, I went to middle school I called myself liking boys and all the kids talked about sex all the time. A bunch of thirteen- year-old kids was talking about how wonderful sex was, and how they felt after their boyfriends was kissing on them. I had seemed to be the only one who didn't have an experience to speak about and at the time I had a boyfriend so I thought. Because everyone else was doing it, I decided to try something new. I was in the eighth grade when I lost my virginity and the boy that I thought was my boyfriend and really liked me, was 17 years old. One day I went over his house and we began kissing and he start to feel on me and you know what happened next: we had sex. Now I thought that this will be

4

# He Was With Me All The Time

something so special and memorable that I will always hold dear to my heart. But instead it was blah and very much boring. In fact, we were in the basement of his house and I was watching television. The boy got so mad at me that he put me out of his house and I walked home. He started telling all his friends that he had a small penis because he was my first and I was watching television. I stayed seven blocks away and I walked home in the dark, so desperate to have love and some kind of affection of someone wanting me that I would put myself in danger by walking in the streets late at night at the age of thirteen. Well when I got home because I hadn't been home from school yet. My mom told me to strip and she beat me on the kitchen floor naked but I couldn't wait to tell everyone what I finally did, I had sex.

I felt like since I did this that I was in with the in-crowd but I was never in. I was only made a fool of because I found out that my so-called boyfriend liked one of my so-called friends. He had told my friend Karen that after he had sex with me he was going to break up with me so that he can date her. All this time that I was with this boy and he never really like me. I was just another piece of tail to him and Karen and all the other people that I hung with knew it. No one told me his plan until after I had sex with him, and once I had sex with him he had tried to talk to Karen but she turned him down so we keep dating. We would continue to have sex and sometimes his brother and sister would stand at the door and listen. That was so degrading, I cared but yet I didn't because any attention at this point was better than no attention. Well how many people know that relationship didn't last?

# He Was With Me All The Time

My relationships from there didn't really get that much better and sex just became a part of a relationship, when God intended for it to be something so much better. There was a lot of negativity in my life growing up as a child. My cousin and their friends would jump on me as a child and just laugh afterwards. They would say man you need to get tough, and all this did was beat me down even farther than I already was. I was in middle school or junior high which ever you will like to call it when I started to smoke marijuana. I use to steal it from my mom's box where she kept her important paper work. Those same friends that knew that my boyfriend really didn't like me and only wanted me for sex, are the same ones that introduced me to marijuana. I use to walk to their house in the morning and from there we would walk to school along with their older cousin.

Every morning walking to school we would get high so by the time the first bell rang for class I was high as a kite. I remember one time I got into an argument with this girl in school, and we decided to go into the girl's bathroom and fight. This girl was one of my friends (supposedly) and as we were in the bathroom fighting another one of the girls that I hung out with jumped on me as well. As if that wasn't bad enough we had another fight in the gym after that and all the girls in that gym jumped on me as well. I developed anger and situations like the fight added to my depression.

In middle school I had a lot of embarrassing moments, but when I got to high school I was so full of anger that it didn't make any sense. I had lost my favorite Aunt Gloria a year before I went to high school. She would always take time to listen and talk to me.

# He Was With Me All The Time

I could talk to her about anything and she always told me the truth. Well except that one time when she had a piece of chocolate on the table and I keep asking for some. She told me to stop begging but I didn't, so she gave me the chocolate and it ended up being an ex-lax. I stayed the next block over from my Aunt house and by the time I got home I was running to the bathroom. Gloria had called my Mom and told her what happened before I got home. After I came out the bathroom my Mom said well I guess that will teach you about begging. My Aunt was the best and I still miss her to this day. When she passed away I was so angry at her because I felt like she was all I had and she left me.

She left me with a crazy family and a mother that I couldn't stand at the time because of all her drinking. I just became even angrier than what I already was. I remember in ninth grade we had a career day and a flight attendant was the speaker. She gave the whole class a blank piece of paper and said do with the paper what you will. But whither you write on it, ball it up, or throw it away you must explain why because that paper represents your life. I took my paper and tore it in half and left the other half blank. The flight attendant said what have you done to your paper and explain why. I told her that I tore it in half because my Aunt had passed and took half of me with her. I didn't feel whole any longer, but the truth was I was never whole in the first place. I left the other half of my paper or my life blank because I felt empty. As a young teenager, I was really crying out only to have no one listen and everyone to go on with their existence as if I said nothing at all. So, from that point on my feeling always remained just that, my feelings.

## He Was With Me All The Time

I dated a few people only to find myself repeating the same things over and over again. I dated this guy in my ninth-grade year and we went out for a little while, about 6 months. Only to find myself back in middle school again, once we had sex he broke up with me and told me that his friend liked me. Well his friend wasn't even thinking about me and didn't like me at all. That was a lie the boy came up with because he didn't want me to think that all he wanted was sex. Here I was dating the same guy (same type of guy) but he had a different name.

## Chapter 3 – Cry for Help, Watch our Words

Running around in the streets all hours of the night trying to be cool and fit in is a cry for help in anyone's world. I had a bad attitude by the time I got to high school, and all my friends that I hung out with had bad attitudes too. I remember getting kick out of school in the ninth grade because we had a big fight in the lunch room. It was about twenty girls and guys that jumped on three girls. We all were kicked out of school and the three girls were number street girls (that was the name of their gang) and the guys from their block came up to the school and shot it up because the girls were jumped on.

Well we left school earlier and by the grace of the living God by the time the guys got up there we had already left not knowing anything about what was going to happen. That situation could have gone way worse than what it did. Someone could have got shot and died, all because of a few words and some girls with bad attitudes. Whoever came up with the saying words don't hurt was a lie, because the truth of the matter is words do hurt. Words are more powerful than what we give them created for. If God could form the earth that we now live, move, and have our being in by words then why can't words hurt? Because of the Word of God being preached people lost their lives including our very own Jesus. Words can make people grow up with low self- esteem and feeling bad about themselves. The words we speak can ignite a fire in you to do harm to someone on a level like you have never thought before.

# He Was With Me All The Time

People are shot over words and they also get beat down physically and mentally all because of the words you chose to speak to someone else. We are all mankind on this earth and together, we should choose our words to build each other up and not tear one another down. The words that you speak out of your mouth can cause people to think about their life and make a positive change. Or it could have them thinking about going to rob a liquor store, and punching someone in the face. The words that you choose to speak to someone can have a long-lasting effect on their lives. It can take people the rest of their lives to try and get over things that has been spoken to them. If a person is always being talked to in a negative way it will shape how they feel about themselves especially in the adolescence stage of life. Because remember this stage is preparing them to become a young adult. By a young person not knowing their worth they will accept, a lot of things that they don't have to accept.

A person who is feed negativity and being beat down by the words of love ones will cause that person to look for acceptance and attention in whom ever will give it to them. It is important for people to know that something that you have spoken to someone in anger out of being hurt, or just being brutally honest has planted a seed in that person mind.

## Chapter 4 – The Pain Gets Deeper

My journey to find love continued and I went out with different guys here and there until I meet James at the mall one weekend. James looked just like Tu- Pac (a rapper) and I was so in love with Tu-Pac because I felt like he understood me. I just could relate to all his anger through his music. James was a grown man and I was still in high school. I dated James for a total of four years, and he was the biggest player there was. The first two years that we dated he wasn't really thinking about me I was (you guess it) another piece of tail.

One day I was talking to James on the phone and it was a lot of people over his house and I heard women talking in the back ground. By this time, I was a senior in high school. My friend had a car and I called her to have her drop me off at James house, but James had no idea I was coming over. My Mom thought that I was spending a night over a friend house. When I first got there this boy that was there didn't want to answer the door and finally James friend Dre' let me in. Everyone was sitting around drinking and smoking marijuana. Well I was first introduced to marijuana in middle school.  I was never much of a drinker but I did smoke weed (marijuana) all the time. I have seen what drinking did to my parents and I didn't want any parts of alcohol. James had a son whose mother was there and of course she was going to make me jealous. The party died down and a lot of people went home.

James and I sat on the coach watching television until Keisha (James son's mother) wanted to talk to him. He goes in the other room with her, and falls asleep on the coach. Keisha has her foot propped up on him and she is sleep too. So now I am at the house by myself looking stupid.

# He Was With Me All The Time

I go in the room where they were and asked him why she had her leg on him? James blew me off and I just went back into the other room and went to sleep. It was only by the grace of God that nothing happened to me over there because who would have care or even tried to help me.

Here I was a child that was dropped off over a grown man house way on the other side of town. These people didn't care about me and I had put myself in a crazy position because my friend went home (that dropped me off over there). It was too late to ride the bus especially by myself so I had no choice but to stay.

The next morning I was on the phone with a guy thinking that would make James jealous but he didn't care one bit. So, I finally told him that I am getting ready to leave and I asked if he would walk me to the bus stop. Well that didn't happen. I walked to the bus stop by myself in a very dangerous neighborhood and went home. Once I got home I called to tell him that I didn't want to be with him anymore. His friend Dre' was in the background laughing at me. I felt so low that words can't even explain. The things that women go through and the position that we put ourselves in some times are so crazy.

I didn't see James anymore for about two years and then he came back into my life, through one of my friends. I tell you the people that I associated myself with and called my friends were nothing but trouble. I really needed to change the company that I kept around me. James and I got back together for another two years, but these two years was so much better than the first. James actually fell in love with me and I became the first person that he ever loved.

# He Was With Me All The Time

He was with me all the time and brought me things and now Keisha was jealous of me. How many people know that if the relationship wasn't healthy the first time around, it wasn't going to be healthy the second time?

I moved out on my own at the age of nineteen, and guess who decided to move in with me? You guess right, James. The good relationship we had changed when James moved in with me. God had blessed me with an apartment, car and new job making good money all in a month time. Those blessings were destroyed by the poor choices that I made. I use to go to work and James would drive my car around all day because he didn't have a job.

He was staying with me and not paying a bill. His friends would come over and eat up my food. They would take showers at my house after they have been out all night cheating on their women. Now what is wrong with this picture? I didn't know my worth and I didn't realize my value, because everything that we had was mine and in my name. But I allowed a man to come in and take control over the blessings that God gave me, so when I lost those things I couldn't really blame him but myself. Now James friends started telling him that they remember when he was the man, but now he has falling off.

They were planting seeds (words) in his mind of how he used to treat women and how much fun it used to be. Now it is ultimately up to James what choice he was going to make, but that depended on the strength that James had stored up in him. So, one night James was picking me up from work and he was high as usual. He claims that he saw an animal in the street and tried to go around it. To keep from hitting an animal and drove my car into a ditch.

# He Was With Me All The Time

The Lord had giving me a vision about my car being in a ditch a month earlier. But I thought that the vision meant for me to stop driving so fast. Just like that the bottom of my car was torn up and I didn't have the money to get it fixed. I didn't even have the money to get it out the ditch at the time. One of my co-workers gave me a hundred dollars to have my car towed out of the ditch. Nothing will teach you a lesson like paying for a car that you no longer can drive. Well I didn't have a car now and I lost my job because I didn't have transportation to get back and forth to work. All this happen after I had already broken up with James because he started to go back to his cheating ways. Shortly after that James got mad at me and moved out.

I have no job or car, James left me and I'm getting ready to lose my apartment, BUT God. Unemployment sent me one check and it was enough to pay my rent for the month. Then I found a job at a donut shop which helped me pay my bills. James was the only person that had ever told me that he loved me.

I was now twenty years old and still in search for some type of love and affection to hold on too. Being angry could not describe how I was feeling after all of this. I developed a hate for James because I felt like everything was his fault, and then he turned around and left me. Bitterness had grabbed a hold of me and leaded me by the hand at this point. I was mad at life, God, James, the job, and my family but I really should have been mad at myself. The blame was placed on any and everybody else but myself. I was the victim but only in my eyes. I was so far into depression that I didn't see a way out.

# He Was With Me All The Time

My family didn't offer me any support to try and help me get back and forth to work, because they were trying to teach me a lesson. James of coarse didn't help me get a car after he lied and said that he would. A hundred dollars was all that I ever saw from him. But how did I expect him to help pay for a car when he barely had a job.

We have to be careful with the choices that we make in life. God had shown me favor and blessed me with desires from my heart. I allowed bad decisions to take everything a way that God had blessed me with. I was back to square one and I was so depressed beyond measure. God gave me signs and warnings so that I wouldn't have to lose anything but I didn't attend to those signs and warnings so I lost everything. I especially lost my peace of mind and crying every night became a second nature to me. Because I cried all the time day in and day out, we need to think about the choices we make and how they can affect us. There is a scripture in the bible that says; (Proverbs 22:6 KJV) Train up a child in the way he should go: and when he is old, he will not depart from it.

Well we need to train our children up in the things of God and in his principles. We as parents need to show them love and a godly character. Therefore, when they get older then will not turn away from the training they have received. If parents do not show their children love and affection where will they get it from? Parents if you never talk to your children about sex who will? My mom has never talked to me about sex but I learned from friends and the streets. That is not training up a child. Mothers if you do not teach your daughters how to be young ladies, who will show them? How will they know what to do? If you never take the time out to talk with them, how will they know that they can come and talk to you.

Look at it this way who are the people they will turn to if you as a parent don't make yourself available to them. We as parents have power to help shape our children into vessels of God at young ages, but the question is will we take out the time to do it? Or are we so busy with other things that we are letting our children pass us by.

## Chapter 5 – The Power of Words

We as parents especially need to be mindful of the words that we speak to our children. We have to be careful not to tear them down. Because out of everyone in the world, parents are the people that they trust the most. If you call your child nothing and no good, then that is how they will see themselves because you are their parent and should know and love them the most. Because I was called fat or tubby all my childhood, when I was older and a lot smaller I still thought that I was fat. Because that it what I was told by my family. So even though my shape was smaller my mind still seen me as being fat. Our words people have power so let's watch how we use them from this day forth.

Even if we see the negative in people especially our children let's choose to build them up with the positive. If truth is told you are only trying to make your children better than you were. You just end up hurting them still. Sometimes we need to sit down and talk with our children and see what they think of us without them getting in trouble. You will be surprised how your children see you as a parent and yet they still love you. Even though it may hurt, hear them and decided to be and do better. I am telling you the invisible images (words) that come out of our mouths are powerful. So, let's use that power to better people. If the foundation is sure the house will stand, this principal is even founded in the kids' classic fairytale "The Three Little Pigs".

Some friends of mine once said "hey let's jump that girl across the street"? Because of that suggestion we went ahead and decided to jump the young lady. Now we really didn't have a reason too, we were just bored and didn't care for her.

# He Was With Me All The Time

We came up with a plan to beat up on the young lady. We went outside across the street and jumped on her. One of the adults from the neighborhood that all the kids got along with and hung out with, seen what we had done and she called us back across the street.

Well as we were running back across the street that young lady went into the house and got a shot gun and pulled the trigger. But by the grace of a merciful God nothing came out even though the gun was loaded. I was the last one to run across the street and if the gun would have fired that young lady would have shot me in the back.

All because someone suggested that we jump on her. Well that night got so much more interesting than just that moment. This same young lady called her family over and they ended up knocking on the door to the house that we were in. Now it was a house full of people and we had guns in the house and they had guns outside. Well thankfully no one was shot, but a lot of arguing and more fighting went on. Just from that one idea that was spoken out of someone mouth. The next time you go to say anything please thinks about it and the effect that it will have on everyone around you.

No one made us fight this girl, and it was our decision to do so. But what I am trying to get you to understand is that our words are seeds that are sown into people lives.

The fruit of the seed sown can cause a path of destruction, especially if the foundation is not sure of the person that the seed is being sown into. When people have no idea who they are or what God has intended for them, they will attach themselves to different things looking for a fit. My family always said negative things but never thought that they were being negative. It was normal to them to say whatever was on their mind. No matter how it would affect the person that they were saying things too. My family felt that you were the one with the problem and you were the weak one if you are effected in a negative way but what was said.

As a child, we were told not to question adults so most of the time the kids never told the parents how they felt about things. We have to listen to our children for they are people too and they have a voice. Just because you are an adult or in charge over someone doesn't give you the right to treat them any kind of way, kids have feelings too.

If your child has issues when they are small and they don't deal with those issues, then they will grow up to be adults with the same problems. God is the ultimate father and yet he listens to us when we go before him in prayer. He (God) doesn't just always talk and we have to listen, for that will not be a conversation. We wouldn't have a relationship.

As parents, we can't be hypocrites especially in front of our own children. But we must show are children the character of God. When our children do not show forth the things that they have been taught, we want to nail them to the cross and crucify them. Because they are making you look bad or you are embarrassed as the parent for what your child has done. When you do that, you forget about the love that Christ shows to us on a daily basis. If truth wore told parents do not handle every situation perfectly. At work when you are acting unseemly you are not showing forth God's character.

# He Was With Me All The Time

When you are super saved in church but outside of church you are lying, cursing, stealing, having sex, have a bad attitude, and gossiping our children watch things like that. They form their own opinions of their parents and most children model after the example that they are shown. Your family is your first ministry and not just in words (do as I say & not as I do principal) but in your actions as well. Think about it are we a people that draw close to God with our lips, but yet are heart (actions, character) are far from him. (Isaiah 29:13 KJV) Does your life style line up with the character of our Savior? What you say you believe in the bible are you living your life according to that or are you just going through the motions and just doing whatever you want too? The best way to teach your children skills, that you want them to have is to possess them yourself.

Look at it this way if you are an individual and the person that you trust and love the most tells you that you are dumb. Then that person will start to think on that or most likely believe that. Especially if it is a mother that is the one tearing down, for you birth the child and you care for that child so if you say that they are dumb, fat or stupid than that is what they will be (or think) because of the position that you hold in their life. Our children are affected by the way we treat them and the words that we say to them. Now all children are not affected in the same way. You can put four children in a room and expose them to the same situation and they all will response differently.

They may be exposed to the same things but because of their individuality they are affected differently. How the situation affected them is what we need to heal, because they will react based on the way they were affected. When your body has an area that is infected it acts differently than normal. Your body is off because of the infection. When you go to the doctor the doctor finds that affected area and then prescribes antibiotics strong enough to fight off the infection. So, that your body can begin it's healing process. It is the same way with hurting people; Christ comes into our lives and applies the antibiotic (His love, The Gospel, Hope) to the affected area (area of hurt) so that the healing process can begin. The problem is we have lived with the infection for so long we have no idea what normal really feels like. Remember to pay attention to the signs of your children and be real with yourself, and them. Your children can't be you but they have to be themselves. God has called them to stand out as individuals.  It is important for parents to allow their children to be themselves and teach them the importance of it. Out of all the people in the world, God only called us to carbon copy of Christ.

# Young Adulthood

## Chapter 6 – Depression Runs Deep

By the time, I reached the stage of young adulthood I was so deep into depression that I would be in a room filled with people and feel so alone. I used to pray and ask for God to just kill me because I felt that I was being tortured by being alive. Most of my nights were spent thinking of ways to kill myself without anyone finding out for weeks.

Depression is not a spirit to play with. It is something that kills you slowly from the inside out. I wouldn't wish it on my worst enemy. Growing up for years with depression and it being the everyday normal is not healthy for anyone to experience. You look for people to fill the void that depression leaves you with. But the fact of the matter is, that only God can pull you out and fill that void in your life. Walking around feeling dead on the inside as depression slowly eats its away to your outside is a trap from the enemy that so many people go through.

I never thought that I would be loved by anyone. The pain and hurt that comes out of that spirit of depression is not easy for someone to understand who's never experienced it. It is not just something that you can get over. People lose their life and everything that is good around them from being depressed. This thing will make you do things that you wouldn't normally do. It will make you sleep with someone else's husband and find it ok. You will start sleeping around just for an inkling of happiness. Other people lives always seem so much better than your own. You function in life until you come across the right moment in time to take your life.

# He Was With Me All The Time

When I got pregnant with my first child I was so deep into depression that it didn't make any sense. I went to all the family dinners and church every Sunday hoping that someone would see through me and hear my soul crying out for help. They never did. It took me getting pregnant to even want to live, even if it was just for a moment.

I didn't want my baby to have to experience all the hurt and pain that I was dealing with. I had so much darkness on the inside of me so why couldn't anyone see it? I often wonder did they see it and just didn't care. The Lord loved on me. He cleaned me up and began to show me Himself. Just like that my life was changed and I was placed on a new path for life.

The bible says "my people are destroyed from lack of knowledge" (Hosea 4:6 KJV), and that was my problem. I had no idea who I was or whom I belonged too. I always tried to fit in with my so-called friends and do the same things that they did but I never fit in. Smoking marijuana, drinking, cursing and having sex was supposed to be fun and the in thing to do when I was growing up. I did those things to fit in but I was only fooling myself. I was destroying myself because I didn't have the knowledge of who I was in Christ. Having a baby made me look past all my hurt and pain and love someone else. I wanted to show her love and build her up so that she would not have to go through all the same things that I went through. See, the problem with people is that we believe we are who everyone else says that we are. But we are who the Lord says we are. It's like Peter in the Bible (Matt 16:18 KJV). He didn't know who he was until God the father revealed who Jesus was to him. Once God showed Peter who Jesus was He could then reveal to Peter who he was. The fact of the matter is that without

24

# He Was With Me All The Time

God we as a people are nothing and can do nothing. In the Lord, we are more than conquerors (Romans 8:37 KJV) in this life. In this life, you will run into people who will try to belittle you and make you feel bad about yourself so that they may feel good about their own lives. The fact is God has made each and every last one of us and he called us good. God has purpose for his people and just because someone doesn't like you or mistreats you doesn't mean that the purpose for your life has ended. Always remember the value of your self-worth is far more priceless and costly than anything on this earth.

You as an individual are so valuable that God sent his only begotten Son to die for you (John 3:16 KJV) so that you can have the right to be connected back to the Father. *Always remember to love yourself.* Out of everyone on this earth no one and nothing thing can ever love you more than Daddy God and Satan's job is to get your focus off of the things of God so that he can come in and destroy you.

Depression is something that is deep in darkness. I am not a doctor and I haven't studied this but it's something that I know firsthand. No pill or drug got me out of that depressed state. It was nothing but the goodness of Jesus and his mercy and grace. The darkness that was on the inside was killing me slowly internally and working its way out to everything around me. It is a secret poison that you don't have to buy and no one can trace it back to a store. I mean I was stuck in my mind. I was stuck in a state of worthlessness. Because I chose to listen to the lies of the devil and all the negative things that people had told me from my childhood it helped contribute to the jail I was living in. The only person who can put you in bondage and keep you there is yourself. People only have the power that you allow them to have, including Satan. Just think. A person can sit around all day and think of ways to die feeling unloved and unwanted by everything and everyone in this life. To walk around and cry oneself to sleep at night is a pitiful state of mind. It just sounds sad and terrible and yet I lived that way every day of my life until age 21. I remember walking around just wanting a hug from someone but never getting it. My spirit was crying out for help but no one heard it or at least didn't care enough to answer the cry.

This experience taught me to listen to the heart of people because their spirit will speak louder than the words they might say any day of the week. I learned compassion for people because of the pain that I experienced in my life. The issue with the church today is that people tend to cover up their hurt and pain when God really wants his people to be healed for real. I am talking about a real personal visitation from God that will change your life like never before. That was what I had experienced and it brought me joy because I was free after being locked up in bondage for years. Just think I walked around for years and most people didn't have a clue that I was in depression and thinking about committing suicide. We are all sisters and brothers in Christ and we need each other. Let's stop tearing one another down and try building one another up.

I looked up Major Depressive Disorder and the things that I found out reminded me of myself as a young adult. Major Depressive Disorder is a mental disorder characterized by an all-encompassing low mood. It is accompanied by low self-esteem and by loss of interest or pleasure in normal enjoyable activities. The term depression itself was derived from the Latin verb *deprimere*, "to press down". From the 14 century "to depress" meant to subjugate or to bring down in spirits.

26

# He Was With Me All The Time

This is what that depression had literally done to me. I was so down in my spirit. I felt like the world was standing on my shoulders pressing me down more.

Major depression significantly affects a person's family, personal relationships, work, school life, sleeping, eating habits and general health. This thing is not just affecting adults but our children are becoming more depressed. Young Adults who are often described as "clinically" depressed feel sad and hopeless or even irritable for weeks or months at a time. In Proverbs 13:12 it says "hope deferred maketh the heart sick". They lose interest in things that they may have at one time enjoyed. Sleeping and eating habits change. Often paying attention can become difficult to do in children that are depressed. This may include watching TV or playing games. Depression is less likely to occur, as well as quicker to remit, among those who are religious as stated in a recent Wikipedia article.

It is not always clear which factors are causes and which are effects of depression. However, depressed persons who are able to reflect upon and challenge their thinking patterns often show improved mood and self-esteem. These are big signs of depression and I displayed them all. When I was in high school I never went to a basketball or football game. I had no interest in any activities. I just went to school and came home. I slept a lot in my young adult stage as well. You could call me anytime of the day and chances are I was sleeping, especially if I was at home. I wasn't enjoying life at all. I was just alive. Let me tell you personally, being alive but not living is miserable. I had a relationship or two where I wasn't treated half bad but I was never satisfied. The truth of the matter was no person could ever satisfy me but I didn't know that at the time.

# He Was With Me All The Time

The reason no one could satisfy me was because I wasn't happy myself. Joy comes from the inside and it runs deep. If you would have looked at me deeply all you would have seen was depression. It's like being in a glass bubble that is filled with darkness and negativity. As you walk around and look at everyone else they all seem happy and you are stuck in this bubble and you have no idea how to get out. Yelling at the top of your lungs while crying for help but at the same time your lips never move. My friends this is what I was living in.

The statement earlier about people who are religious and how depression is less likely to occur very well may have some truth to it. But I have always been in church and I was deep into this depressed state. However, when I started to develop a relationship with God my world changed. Please pay attention to the signs of your loved ones, children, co-workers and even yourself. If you notice that people around you seem depressed, please don't pass them by every day and not try to make a difference. We have to help one another and stop just worrying about ourselves.

A kind word or a hug from the heart can help someone in depression so much. Remember there were times when I just wanted a hug. I would have broken down into tears and that would have been a form of release for all the pain that was bottled inside. It would have told someone that something was going on with me. Why didn't I just tell somebody? In my mind, no one cared so why tell anyone. You may read this and say am I my brother's keeper? To a certain degree yes you are.

## Chapter 7 – Loneliness

Wikipedia describes loneliness as unpleasant feelings in which a person experiences a strong sense of emptiness and solitude resulting from inadequate levels of social relationships. However, it is a subjective experience. Loneliness has also been described as social pain - a psychological mechanism meant to alert an individual of isolation and motivate her/him to seek social connections.

I want you to notice how it still deals with pain because pain has a lot to do with the different emotions we experience throughout our life time. Christ died so that we as a people could be free and in right standing with the Father but somewhere along the lines this information has been twisted up or not fully understood. When you take your eyes off God and focus them on your present situation then you tend to ignore God and take things into your own hands. Sex before marriage is something that the bible speaks against. It is a sin (missing the mark) and the Father knows that sin leads to death, spiritual and possibly even physical death. Think about it. If we were obedient to the things of God there would be no single parents, no sexual disease, no blended families, no sexual strong holds, etc. because we would wait until we were married.

We are under grace and mercy. We have the ability to repent of our sins and move on so that we can be connected to the father. This is not a license to go out and sin and do whatever we want thinking that God will just forgive us. There comes a time in life that we have to grow up naturally and spiritually. Sex is a gift from God that was set up for the husband and the wife. The first time that sex is experienced by a husband and wife there should be a shedding of blood.

# He Was With Me All The Time

This is to bind the union together in a covenant. It is why women bleed when they have sex for the first time. It is meant to be a contract with your husband. Just because a person is single doesn't mean that the person is lonely in terms of a relationship. So why do people feel alone and by themselves? Sometimes we look at other people's situations and say within ourselves that we want that kind of happiness. Loneliness is something that usually attacks people with self-esteem issues. We all can feel alone from time to time but I am talking about loneliness. I hung out with a lot of people when I was younger and I would still feel alone. I believe that loneliness is not a root of its own. What do I mean by that? I believe that there is a deeper root within and loneliness is a stem of the deeper issue. For instance, you may be depressed or have low self-esteem and loneliness is a stem from those other issues.

There are so many people on this earth that have a sense of loneliness and they walk around feeling so alone. It seems as if everyone in life is constantly on the go, always moving, because people are so busy. We are too busy. We are passing by our children, husbands, wives, loved ones and the people that we see on a daily basis. The people who probably suffer from these things the most. Let's slow down because honestly, we are busy doing nothing. Always on the go to go nowhere when someone around us needs to know that they are loved and special. At the end of the day when you look up, what have you accomplished in life besides paying your bills?

The other day I told a co-worker of mine that there is more to our life than just getting up going to work, church, school, and home, doing the same things over and over again day after day. Where have we made a difference?

## He Was With Me All The Time

Whose life have we made an impact on? As Christians, we should impact people's lives daily and show forth the love of Christ. People shouldn't feel lonely in a world filled with people. When you find, yourself sitting around and feeling lonely then get up and go and positively impact someone else life on purpose. You will find that as you are making a difference in someone else's life you are truly being fulfilled in your own life as well. Always remember that you are never alone because God will never leave you or forsake you (Hebrews 3:5, KJV).

## Chapter 8 – Abused, Hurt & Having Sex

I used to have a very bad attitude to the point that my Mom would talk to me about it. She said that she could see me ending up dead or in jail. That attitude came out of the hurt and pain that I had experienced at an earlier age. I am not making excuses for people who do have a bad attitude. I want others to keep in mind that you never know why someone acts the way they do. Hurt that is covered up can never be dealt with.

Even when you go to the doctor you are asked to show where the pain is located and at what number would you rate your pain. Where the pain is, will be the spot that the doctor starts to examine. How high you rate the pain tells the doctor how severe the pain is. The doctor goes to the root of the problem once you let him know where that problem lies. The Lord knows all but He is waiting on you to acknowledge the problem for yourself. Being real with yourself and others makes you accountable for your life and the things that you deal with. I believe that is why people walk around covering up a lot of things because they don't want to be accountable.

Take a look at yourself and be honest enough to say how high you would rate your pain. You have to deal with pain head on. It is not something that will just leave by itself. People who have really bad attitudes are people who are filled with hurt and pain. Attitudes are cries for help. We need to learn how to recognize these cries and deal with them because hurt people, hurt people. There is so much hurt and pain that people go through. They have learned to function with dysfunction. There are functioning depressed people walking about on a day to day basis. People go through years of pain that they began experiencing in their childhood. So, by the time they come into adulthood they are not sure how to inform people that they are hurting. The pain that has been suppressed into their memories, the real source of the pain, is not known to the person operating in it. I have gone through a lot of trials throughout my life. I have learned not to judge people but to try and understand the root of the problem. This lesson was taught to me by the things that I went through in my own life. We have to be like the nozzle on the root killer bottle. The Holy Ghost will be the root killer and we need to go to the root of the issues.

I used to have a friend that was very abusive to her boyfriend. When they would argue, she would always hit on him. Most people are abused behind closed doors. But with her wherever they were that is where the abuse took place. What most people didn't know was she was abused by her last boyfriend for a few years. He was very controlling and he used to hit on her all the time. No matter how much we would tell her to leave him she never did. It actually took for him to go to jail for her to leave him. Even though he was abusive it seemed she loved him even more. She would do anything for him and jumped at his every request. So many excuses were made on his behalf as if he was the victim. The sad part is he was a victim in a different situation that caused him to act the way he did. About nine months after the young man went to jail she started dating one of his friends. This friend is the one who she used to abuse. She would charge after him with bottles and throwing things at him. We asked her to stop doing things like that, but she refused. He never hit her back. He would just leave. One day we were all over her mom's house and they got into another argument. She went charging at him again and she almost knocked over their new born baby in the bassinet. We had to grab the bassinet to protect the baby. All she saw was rage because she just kept charging after him. After that moment, we told her that if they moved in together he would probably abuse her because he would come to the point that he was tired. Believe me when I tell you I do not encourage abuse in any form. They did move in together and he took her all the way to the Westside of town. My friend was gone all of a month before she was back home with her mom because one night he was tired and he hit her back. It may seem funny to some people but the truth is it was a cycle of one hurt person that abused another hurt person who abused another hurt person. The reality that women are abusing men is real. There are women out there who are being abused by men also. No abuse should be overlooked. It is all wrong. We are all valuable in the sight of the Lord. There was even a point when my friend only felt loved when the first boyfriend was hitting on her.

I have never had to deal with physical abuse but I know so many women personally who have. I have dealt a lot with verbal abuse from childhood through adulthood. Man, you have no idea of the affect it had on me. I read an article that was talking about verbal abuse. The article said that a person who feels they are being attacked by someone who is verbally abusive on a regular basis should seek professional counsel. They should remove themselves from the negative environment whenever possible. How do you as a child remove yourself from your parent's verbal abuse? Staying with someone who is verbally abusive is damaging for a person's well-being. Despite being the most common form of abuse, verbal abuse is generally not taken as seriously. The reason being is, there is no visible proof and the abuser may have a perfect persona around others. However, verbal abuse can be more detrimental to a person's health than physical abuse. If a person is verbally abused from childhood on, he or she may develop psychological disorders that plague them into and throughout adulthood. This helped me to understand why I was so depressed for years. The article went on further to say that after exposure to verbal abuse victims may fall into clinical depression or post-traumatic stress disorder. The person targeted by verbal abuse over time may succumb to any stress related illness. Verbal abuse creates emotional pain and mental anguish in its targets. This was something that I found out first hand.

Any form of abuse can leave children to grow up and become struggling adults in their emotions and mentally. This is why I try to be careful with how I speak to my children and others because I am aware of the damage it can cause. There are times when I want to say things to hurt others but I chose to think about it and how it will affect them. Let's love more and not hurt each other so much. Let's learn how to have compassion on others. It was difficult to understand that I was being abused as a child. As a matter of fact, I didn't realize that I was abused until my adulthood. I just thought that it was a way of life. I ask my children, one day in a conversion we were having. "Why is it the norm for siblings to argue and fight all the time? Why do we consider that normal? Why can't the normal be for everyone to get along and love each other without saying things to make the other feel bad?" Verbal abuse is best described as a negative defining statement told to you about you. Watch out for the signs of verbal abuse. It is any negative thing that someone is defining you by or telling you that is who you are: you are dumb, stupid, fat, etc. Even Satan's attack on believers is verbally abusive. It is the things that he tries to plant in our hearts. Please watch out how you define others and yourself for that matter. Don't let other people's definition of you affect what you think about yourself. Any form of abuse can cause a person to reach out for other things as a since of fulfillment such as drugs, sex, or alcohol to name a few.

So, we have women that have gone through childhood abuse. Some of those same women have been physically abused and some are abusing others. Some of these women get into relationships with men and sleep around. Women- you don't have to lay down with everyone and give your body away. Your body is priceless. It is so priceless that Jesus shed his blood for it. The scripture reads in 1 Corinthians 3:16 KJV "Know ye not that ye are the temple of God, and that the Spirit of God dwelleth in you?" As women, we desire to be married but by the time we finally get to our husbands we are so full of different men and hurt that we don't know who we are. What am I talking about? Every time you sleep with someone that man deposits some of himself into you. Without even realizing it you can begin to take on some of his traits. You may also compare your husband to past sexual experiences and if, in your eyes, he doesn't measure up then you now have a problem in the bedroom with your mate. This was not Gods intent for the marriage bed.

We wouldn't have to experience these issues if it wasn't for the fall from the Garden of Eden and the fall in our personal walk with the Father. Sex in general is not a sin. It becomes a sin

# He Was With Me All The Time

when you have it with someone that is not your husband. There is an intimacy that a husband and wife should develop before they even have sex. This intimate place will cause your sex life to be great with your husband. When you are in relationships with people and they pressure you into having sex with them and you do, it takes you out the will of God. There are even those who are not pressured into it but they are the one who is pressuring someone else.

The demonic world has taken something truly precious by God and perverted it. We have Christian brothers involved with pornography and dirty magazines. Pastors and ministers are sleeping with women in the congregation. It even goes as far as people in different countries paying for human trafficking. There are prostitutes on the street selling their bodies trying to make money for their family. Women are stripping trying to pay for college. There are women in the body of Christ that are prostituting themselves and they are not on the streets. Some of these women haven't even realized that they are a prostitute and money is their pimp. All of this is still relative to sex and the desire and extremes that people go through to get it. Sin is sin whether you are having sex with your boyfriend or you are on the corner selling your body to a stranger. Please think about this the next time you ride pass a prostitute. Think before you put on your judgment hat with your bracelet to match that says I am better than her. We have to stop covering up things and trying to make it ok when God has called his people to a higher way. Women you are more than just your figure.

You have more going for you than just your shape. Think about the talent of a woman and how strong we are as individuals. The fact of the matter is that the experiences we had in our childhood on through adulthood have shaped our insecurities, cause us to build walls and harbored hurts that we still walk around with today. No matter what you've gone through in life you are fearfully and wonderfully made. We can't get mad at God for everything that went wrong, or is going wrong in life that we've experienced. We have to learn how to seek and ask for his guidance in dealing with the things that we are dealing with. We have to see the problem and grab it by the horns to pull it down so that it won't latch on to our children and follow us into our marriages.

When you go through your childhood being verbally abused and you walk into young adulthood empty and depressed, where do you go from there? Who can you turn to? Who can you trust when the people you trusted the most have mistreated you? I found my trust in God. My Mom never told me that she loved me. I asked her about that one time. Her response was I used to tell you all the time but when you turned about 2 or 3 you didn't like for me to say that to you, so I stopped. My father was never there for me and I went through so much hurt going through that situation alone. One day God said to me at a young age that my mom couldn't show me something that she never received herself. If no one ever showed you love or you never experienced someone showing you how much they loved you, then how do you know how to give it? When I was a little older and I learned more about. God I realized that even though my father wasn't there I had to still respect him as my father and I would be alright in God eyes. I later found out that my mom was abused as a child in a way that I never was. The hurt and pain she experienced was never dealt with. How could things have been different in her life? Can you image how she could have touched her kids if healing would have taken place

# He Was With Me All The Time

after the hurt? That is truly something to think about because no matter how old you are, there is still a chance for deliverance. God has truly helped me through a lot of things in life. He has freed me from some issues that I was struggling with. I still battle certain things here and there. The pain, hurt, disappointment, and everything else I've gone through helped shape me into the person that I am today. Because of what I went through I recognize the signs in my children or a co-worker and I can encourage them. I have more compassion for people. I can truly say that I have learned from my mistakes and from the one's my parents made as well.

I remember growing up and all the adults were drunk and the kids were basically just left to fend for themselves. One time all the adults were drunk and we were all outside late at night. One of the ladies threw her cigarette on the ground and I decided to go and pick it up to have a smoke. I thought that was cool back in the day. My older sister gave me a whipping that I've never forgotten. I have never smoked a cigarette from that day to this one. I had sex at a young age when I should have enjoyed being a child. In school I fought all the time because I was so angry. As I said before I remember when I first came to Detroit my cousins used to fight me every day (they said that they were making me tough). My mom would say go and fight back or I am going to fight you. Then when I got kicked out of school all the time for fighting she couldn't figure out why.

Well she was the one that told me to fight. I was called names my whole life. My mom always worked afternoons or midnights so my older brother would watch me (I guess that is what he thought he was doing) but I had too much freedom and not enough time spent with my mom. I went through all that and a whole lot more. God has truly been good to me and he has been with me all the time. God is with you too, carrying and covering you every step of the way. As the Lord was healing my heart from all hurt and pain I discovered a world that I had not known before, a world that had peace. I could sleep at night. I started to develop respect for myself and learned to say no to men who just wanted to use me.

 The truth of the matter is most men want the good girl to take home to his parents and marry. The other girls are just for sex and a little fun. At one time, I had a fling with a married man. He never wore his wedding ring. One day we were lying in the bed and I asked him, "Why don't you wear your ring?" It truly bothered me that this was someone else's husband that was in my bed. He said, "I just don't." Then I asked, "If you are married then why are you out here in these streets?" He said, "Just in case no one in these streets wants me I have someone at home." All the time I was feeling bad that I was messing with this man.  I was in such a state that any man probably would have done the trick to tell the truth.  I knew a lot of people that dated married men. It was just a way of life to be honest. It bothered my spirit so much that I ran him off with all the questions. Truly my character was not to sleep with another woman's husband but that is what I found myself doing, because I just needed someone to take interest in me.

Knowing your worth as an individual will keep you from falling into relationships with someone else's husband. One thing is for sure that when he left I wasn't upset. I just didn't know how to say that I didn't want that fling. I learned not to judge people because they don't act like we want them too. You never know why people do what they do or why they act the way they do. It's time out for putting on new clothing over the old mess. God is real and not fake. What he wants to do in your life can happen if you allow it to. When you get to the point that you are truly sick of being tired you will do something different. An example of a person that is insane is someone doing the same thing but expecting different results.

If we want different results, then we have to do something different. When I got in Christ and found out that I wasn't a mistake, and that God had a plan for my life since the foundation of the world, it blew my mind. The day that I accepted the Lord as my personal Savior and desired a relationship with him was the day my life changed. I had been in church all my life but I didn't make him my Savior until I was in my early twenties. I had already said the prayer of salvation but I am talking about when I truly accepted Him in my life.

I knew of God but I had no idea who he was. I was in my apartment and I told the Lord that I wanted to know him for myself. I said, "Lord first before I truly decide to walk this Christian walk for real is there anyone who can do this?" All I had ever seen was hypocrites. The Lord answered me and said yes. I asked, "Was there anyone in my life?" He showed me my god-mother and how she always lived the same way before him every day of the week.

Then I told the Lord that if I did this walk then I didn't want to know the Lord of my mom, god-mom, or grandmother, but I wanted to know him for myself. Along this journey, I have gotten to know him for myself. I don't ride on other people's testimonies but mine. I have seen his hand upon my life and I have had an encounter with him that has changed my life forever. We have been created by God and he calls us good. So, no matter what you have been told all your life, know that you are wonderful. You will have a fight on your hands when you try to change the way you think. However, it is so worth it. You are alive so know that you can have better in your life. No matter what stage of life you are in deal with the issues and make the necessary changes. Talk to yourself in the mirror every day and tell yourself how special you are. Hold your head up and stand strong. Be encouraged in who you are and embrace being unique.

# Motherhood

## Chapter 9 – Motherhood

Most people recognize a Mom as someone who has birthed out a child. I looked up the word motherhood and it does involve birthing of some sort whither you are birthing something spiritually or naturally. The funny thing about the whole birthing process is that whatever baby you are carrying (child, business, book or even a ministry) it has to go through a process of growth and development before it can be fully birth out.

In the natural as the baby is growing and preparing for birth, some moms are reading and learning about what will take place during the delivery and what they should do afterwards. Then you have other parents who are doing nothing but waiting on the baby to be born. What do I mean by that? I mean that anytime you are pregnant you should learn about what is going on inside of you, and what are the different stages that your baby will go through. Also, study up on the delivery process and what colors will stimulate the baby's mind, and keep those colors around your baby. In the spirit, you are not always sure what all you will have to go through to birth out your baby. But you should get your instructions from the Lord and directions on what to do. I remember when I was pregnant with my first baby I didn't look up any information on what I was getting ready to go through. I was one of the ones who just had a baby. I went from being at my lowest point in life at the time to being pregnant with a baby. Before I found out that I was pregnant I remember asking God could my life get any worse. Then I found out that I was with child and I thought oh yes it can get a whole lot worse. How in the world was I going to raise a child I was barely taken care of myself? I had no idea that this baby girl I was caring would help change my life around. What I thought was a disaster end up being a blessing (I never thought that the baby was a disaster but the whole part of me being the mother). Well with this new experience of motherhood I started to cry a new tune unto the Lord about helping me live. Now I had something to live for. You have to remember that I was depressed all my life up until this point of becoming someone's Mom. God came and snatched me right out of that darkness. The Lord loved on me, cleaned me up and began to show me Himself. Just like that my life was changed and I was place on a new path for life. I wanted to show my baby love like never before and I wanted the best for her. Things I didn't have when I was a child I wanted to bless her with.

My first child I nickname her my world changer. Because she changed my world and life without her is something that I can't even imagine. When things seemed to be out of our control we must go to the father (God) for direction and instruction. This is something that we should have been doing anyway. We as a people wait until there is a problem before we seek for a solution. Sometimes we even wait until there is a problem to even talk to the father. He is waiting on us to come in fellowship with him. The Lord can use any situation to make it work out for your good. Like the scripture, says "And we know that **all things work together for good** to them that love God, to them who are the called according to his purpose" (Romans 8:28 KJV).

Now being a single parent and trying to work and raise a child or children is not very easy to do. However, it can be done. When I was a single mother before my husband and I was married, it was hard working and raising a daughter. When you are single everything falls on you and you don't have that support that you need and desperately want.

# He Was With Me All The Time

Sometimes when you are married everything can still fall on you and you have another body there that can be a support system. The bible talks about how God can do exceedingly and abundantly above all that we may ask or think according to the power that works on the inside of us (EPH 3:20 KJV). Well that power is the Holy Spirit and all we have to do is ask or think about being a good parent and God can exceed that expectation in our lives. It is very important for the parent to have a healing process with the Lord with whatever hurt that they are dealing with especially if it concerns the father of that child.

After the pain, you may develop bitterness and sometimes take it out on the child. There are mothers that are so frustrated because they are a single parent and they feel like the weight of the world is on their shoulders. They are walking around hollering at the child all the time unleashing their frustration out on the one they love the most. As adults, sometimes we think that are problems and issues only affects us. When in fact the truth is that it affects everyone around us especially are children. Because of all the hurt and pain my Mom went through as a child and never had healing taken place in her it affected how she showed love. We need are mothers and our woman to walk in total healing and victory in their lives, because the world needs them. Women are beautiful creatures that God has made on this earth; we have the ability to do so many great and wonderful things. There are so many of us that hold a huge roll in life and at times it can be so overwhelming. We are called to be mothers, wives, friends, co-workers, cooks, housekeepers, teachers, spiritual leaders, sisters, daughters, counselors, and vision pushers.

# He Was With Me All The Time

We are expected to be a lot of things to a lot of people and still somehow some way keep a little time for ourselves. We are able to do all that and still have time to ourselves. We need to allow God a chance to truly be God and Lord over our lives. He can help and guide us in every way. After God made man (Adam) he said that it is not good for man to be alone but that he will make a help meet for him (Genesis 2:18 KJV). We are not only help meets for our husbands but we are to be helpers to all those that are around us. Nonetheless we can't get so caught up in helping others that you forget about your own family. Tell your sons and daughters how much they mean to you, and who they are in God. Let them know why you discipline them, why you push them so hard; The things that you have experienced in your life time, be honest enough with yourself to be honest with them. You will find out that it will help them along the way.

They won't feel so alone in life because they will know that you have walked through what they are going through. Let them know that you had sex too soon and that you really don't know how to express yourself. We not only as women but as a body of Christ have to be honest with ourselves and others. Take off the mask come from behind the curtains and be truly naked before the Lord. For the Lord wants you healed for real. Tell your girl friends that you are not sure how to really be a good friend to someone; to have patience with you as you learn along the way. We are all going through different things and have different struggles that we face in life. We need each other, you can't do it alone and you are not superwoman because she doesn't exist. Learn the word no in the right seasons and yes in the right moments. Tell your husband that you just want a hug and let him know that you want him to listen to you.

Tell your Mom's that you want more time with them, and your Dads to show you what you should look for in a man. Once you face your biggest problems, facing others will be easy. Many of our biggest problem is ourselves. We can't be honest with ourselves because then we will have nothing to hind behind anymore. Some have worn mask for so long that they have started to believe the lie that they tell them ourselves. Be honest with yourself and be free. I understand that it is not easy to deal with the parts of ourselves that as not right. But it is very much important. The only way to grow is to deal with the you, that you do not want to deal with. I tell my daughter all the time, "don't fool yourself". Many times, we are fooling others and haven't realized that we have fooled ourselves in the process.

If you dig deep within yourself and pull out the strength that you need to face your issues with yourself head on, then it will become easier when others bring up things about yourself that they are not happy with. You owe it to yourself to be the best version of you that you can be, and we all have the strength within us. Most are just not willing to face themselves. You can decide today that I am going to face myself and deal with the things that I see that I'm not pleased with. Your goal in this, is to be free. I charge you today, to be free. Because you already are, whither you know it or not.

## Chapter 10 - Freedom

Ask God to show you who you really are in him. Inquire of God to show you people that you need to let go. Tell God that you need his assist in letting go of things that are not good for you. It is ok for you to be seen (without walls) because people see you anyway and you are the one who doesn't see yourself. What I mean by that is people put up walls and they act a certain way trying to cover up who they really are and the hurt that is on the inside of them. But people see the hurt and they see why you act the way you do so the only person that you are kidding is yourself. God sent his only begotten son to be delivered up for us so that we can be connected back to the Father. So why do we think that he (God) doesn't care about our well-being. The Lord loves you and he wants the best for you. Our God is a good God and he cares about you and your happiness. Please don't allow the spirit of deception to attack your minds to think that God Almighty doesn't care about you. The battle of this spiritual war is in your minds and we as a people need to do what the bible has instructed for us to fight this war. You will be surprised how many people have no idea that God loves them.

Even though everyone knows the scripture (John 3:16 KJV) "for God so loved the world that he gave his only begotten Son, that whosoever believeth in him should not perish but have everlasting life". However, what I have found out is that when you read the Word of God, that you have to read it slow enough for the living Word to come alive in you, and you should always personalize it. So, you should read the scripture like this: "for God so loved (me) that he gave his only begotten Son, that whosoever (that when I) believeth in him (I) should not perish but have everlasting life". You are not taking out words or adding to the scripture but you are simply making it personal; So, that you can have a life changing experience with the Creator. I find it hard to believe that people have experience Christ or came into His presence when nothing about you have changed. Something is very wrong with that picture. Because every time I have been in the presence of God I have been broken before him. I have walked away different. Whenever people have had an encounter with Jesus in the bible they never walked away from him the same. Something about them had changed. If we as the children of God can't be honest with our father than who can we been honest with? How can we walk in the freedom that was given to us?

Take time with the Father in pray so that you can know who you are in him. We all are precious jewels in him but do you know which one you are? Everybody is not a diamond and all are not rubies. Spending time with the Father will let you know who you are. There are much more gems out there that do not get recognize because everyone wants to be something that they are not. Maybe you are not functioning properly because you're trying to be something that you are not. You have to be you and allow other people to be themselves. Think about it this way if we all were the same, then someone wouldn't be needed. For example, you have different worship leaders that may have similar gifts but their different styles of worship are blessing us in different ways. What if Elijah (in the bible) was trying to be Isaiah then Elijah wouldn't be needed. Because Elijah was Elijah and Isaiah was Isaiah then both were needed for the Kingdom of God. They both were used for the Glory of God. Two powerful prophets and they had similar gifts but yet they were still different. I don't understand why people do not want to be different. Think back to when you were a child and you realized that you were different from your friends. The first thing you did was try to be like them. You wanted to dress how they dressed and look how they looked, not realizing who you are. Being different is who we are and who we are called to be, we are not all the same. God is so amazing that he can take us and shape us into the same form but yet be different.

We all have hands and figure prints but out of all the people in the universe no two fingerprints are the same. Wow! Only God can do that. Take identical twins that look exactly the same, move the same, and may even talk the same and I will show you two completely different people. Embrace who you are and know who you are in Christ. The only person that you have to be is yourself to be successful. It is when you try to be someone else or someone you are not that makes you a failure. Why are you a failure? Because you have failed yourself before you even tried to be you. You don't even know what you are capable of doing or being. Seeing how you haven't given yourself a chance. There are so many of our love ones walking around thinking that they are a mistake in life. Well the devil is a liar, you are not a mistake you were called to be alive so that you can bring Glory to God. Therefore, you are the only one who can do your part in that. I once heard a pastor say out of the millions of sperm that flowed through your Mom you where the one that came forth.

When I heard that it changed how I thought about myself. I was no longer a mistake but I was destined and I have a purpose. No one is on earth just to roam around and try to figure out who they are. We all have a purpose and can bring glory to God's kingdom. We have to learn to cast down our thoughts. Just because something pops into your mind, doesn't mean that the thought is how you really feel. Also, remember that you have a choice to act on what you think or to cast that thought down. Why would we believe anything that the devil says anyway? He is the father of lies and he has lied from the beginning? We have weapons against the enemy and our weapons are mighty through God (2 COR 10:4-5 KJV). You have the ability to throw those thoughts down when they come. As a Christian you can never fully be who you are until you first make up in your mind that you want to be saved. What do I mean by that? Well you can't be a saint and a sinner at the same time; you have to choose which one you are going to be.

You have the power to choose because God gave it to you. It is called a free will. In the book of Revelation, it talks about (Rev 3:15-16 KJV) how you have to be hot (saved) or cold (of the world), because if you are lukewarm then the Lord will vomit (spew) you up out of his mouth. Exactly how can you live for God (when you want too) on Sundays but then the rest of the week you are so full of junk and mess. To the point that no one even knows that you are saved, until you open your mouth and say that you are saved. You wonder why your friends won't come to church with you. Let me help you, it's because you are showing forth bipolar disease in the natural, who are you really and what do you stand for? You can't just talk about this thing but you have to live this life out on a daily basis. The sad part is some of you are leaders in the church spreading that spirit (deception) to other people. I am not trying to convict you, but the Holy Spirit needs you to see the error of your ways. That you can change and grow up into the things of God and walk in a mature (perfect) nature. God wants to do great things for you, in you and through you. We won't allow Him the opportunity to work totally in us. The mind can be a tricky place; I remember there were certain times in my life where I felt that if I thought on something long enough that I would have a nervous breakdown. I would change my thought patterns and think on the goodness of God (Phil 4:8). I found out that just because things enter into your mind doesn't mean that you have to go through with the whole thought. Everything that pops up into your mind isn't necessary you.

I began to see things in a different light. I use to think that if I thought about something that it was me (my true feelings). However, the devil is big on suggestions. He throws something into your mind and you meditate (think of them continually) on it long enough, then you will most likely do what you have thought on. For example, if someone does something to you in a negative matter. You keep rehearsing (thinking) the situation in your mind, you will build anger. Maybe even resentment, but you will get to a point where you act on that thing. Women, mother, daughter, sister, and friend remember this; God has created you and he created you for his purpose and glory so know that there is more to you than what you see. God didn't bring you into the world without first calling you good. He will take care of. You are beautiful and you are very precious in the sight of God. Know your worth and get a relationship with your daddy to find out that you are royalty.

I don't care what you are going through and what you may be facing right now in life. You are not a mistake and you were meant to be here. Nothing and no one, nowhere on this earth will (or could) ever love you like the great I AM (God). Out of everyone that has ever said the words "I love you", He is the one that loves you the most. God has selfless (agape) love for his children that no matter what, you will always be loved by God. As a matter of fact, think of one person that you love more than anything on this world or in this life and God loves you more than that. I truly can't stress enough how much you are loved by God. There are so many of his children walking around in the world, who truly don't know that God loves them. When things go wrong in this life most people want to blame God. But like I tell my children no matter what you do in life whether good or bad there is a consequence. If you do well (good) then you will reap the consequence for that, but if you do badly then you will reap the consequence for that so it is your choice.

Next time you look in the mirror hold your head up and speak to yourself. Tell yourself that you are righteous in Christ Jesus and that you are beautiful. Whether you believe it or not people can pick up how you feel about yourself if they stay around you long enough. Also, you give off a signal to men based on your self-esteem level. The esteem you have about yourself (either low esteem or high esteem) is seen by the way you dress, speak, and just your overall appearance. Your net worth is so great of a price that God had to send his Son Jesus to purchase you back for him (God). The next time you think that you are not worth anything or the devil tries to plant lies in your mind, please remember who you are.

Your value is so high that nothing on this earth could purchase you, but the blood of Jesus. Be comfortable with yourself, and who you are in Christ. People do not spend time with themselves let alone God to know who they really are. In Matt 16 (verse 18) Peter didn't know who he was until he first spent time with God and then God gave him revelation about Jesus. Then Jesus in return gave Peter revelation about Peter. There is no telling how Peter saw himself before that revelation came to him. How do you see yourself? I bet if you spent more time with God you will review yourself differently. God is your father and he will and is waiting to speak into you just like a natural father would do. If a young woman had a father pour into her and treat her like a princess (that she is) then she will look for nothing less than that in a mate. But if a woman didn't have someone pour into her, then the first person that shows her a little of attention she will fall for. No matter what we go through in life God has already made provisions for us to overcome that thing. We have victory in Him but if we never get in him (not know of him) then how can we obtain our victory.

Do not allow your hardships, experiences and past relationships cause you to form an opinion of who you are. You are a child of the King that is above all kings. You my sister are royalty a real-life princess that is who you are. We will never be better than each other (women) because we have the same father. However, you will always have rule over darkness. Know who you belong too because as a member of the royal family you have authority. Sisters in Christ you are not what others say that you are and you are not what you can do (talent).

The Lord once asked me "who are you?" not what can you do or what gift I gave you but do you know who you are? He said because if I strip your gifts away from you today you will still be royalty, simply because you are my daughter and I Am the

King of all kings. When Boas asked Ruth, who are you? Ruth said it so profoundly, she said 'I am Ruth'.

Royalty is inherited you can't work for it but you are born into it. When you accept, what Christ has done for you on the cross then you became born into this royal family. I really want you guys to get this because you are special and you need to know this. If you don't know that you are special, then you will allow yourself to continue to be treated any kind of way. Yet you are a princess and you deserve the best. We need to learn how to enjoy the different stages in our life whither it is the process that we go through or the promise. The fact is God is faithful and he will do exactly what he promised to do. Now the process will grow us and we will learn and are developed in the process before we ever reach the promise. It's because of who you were made into (created) by the process that you can enjoy the promise. The things that you learned on the way to the promise are what are important. Because those things have created you into the person that you are. When I were a child I use too dream big and dream all the time. But as life went on I stopped dreaming and just started existing. The more I found out about God, the more I think about my life. I am starting to realize that I don't just want to exist but I want more out of life. The better part of life so to speak, is not for the other people but for anyone who goes after it. There are so many people out there that look up to famous people and athletes.

Yet they don't realize what is on the inside of themselves. We are exceptional creatures and there is nothing on this earth that can compare to us. Because we are made in the image and

# He Was With Me All The Time

likeness of father God. Out of everything that he made we are the only beings that can speak, decree, and flow in authority.

We are not to beat others down to make ourselves look good (only in our eyes) but we are individuals and we need to stand out individually. Each of us has amazing talents and gifts that can change this very world that we live in. A lot of times we are so busy wishing for someone else's life that we do not enjoy our own. We can never love effectively when we don't know how to love ourselves. With that being said we need to face our problems, fears, and pain head on. We need to be accountable for what we do and say in life. We need to know if we are influencing people to be the best that they can be. Being accountable is not easy to do but it can be done. I once heard John Bevere speak about living an extraordinary life and the message was so powerful. I wonder how many people grabbed a whole of that message and went to walk on in the grace of God. We as a people have been made free through Jesus but if you don't know that you are free, how will you walk in it. We have to believe the bible and walk in everything that God said that we can have. We have to spend time with God to know who we are in him. You will learn how we are a people of great value. Whither anyone ever tell you or not. If you never had anyone tell you how wonderful you are let me do it right now. You (put your name here) are beautiful you are special, a precious gem, and you are loved so much. You (put your name here) are the apple of God's eye and anyone will be lucky to have you as a mate.

Everything about you is radiant from the top of your head to the bottom of your feet. You (put your name here) are so smart and you are brave because of what you put into your children they will succeed. If you take nothing from this book take that with you and hang on to it for the rest of your life. Believe in yourself and follow hard after your dreams.

Believe in yourself and don't allow other people beliefs of you become your reality. What I love about father God is that when he looks at us he sees the person that we can be. Based on the things that are placed on the inside of us. The thing of the matter is you can do more and be more than what you are right now. Let's think about this right now, the Creator of anything and every living thing that you see has designed you. He has created you and placed his spirit on the inside of you. God has delivered up his only begotten son to come to this sinful world and die for you. So, what do you think that God won't do for you? The power to succeed is on the inside of you and God loves us with a sacrificial love. The point that I keep trying to drive home is that because the Father loves us we can do anything that we set out to do.

Believe in yourself and push yourself to go for the gusto. You can focus on the finish to achieve the goal, that you have in mind for yourself. Whatever your goals are you can make them happen from the smallest goal to the largest. The only person that can hold you down is yourself. It is like I told my husband, the only time you have failed is when you haven't even tried. Even if you try at one thing you keep trying until you make it happen. Success is on the inside of your belly and you have the power to succeed at whatever you do.

I am reminded of the scripture that says "Trust in the LORD with all thine heart; and lean not unto thine own understanding.

# He Was With Me All The Time

In all thy ways acknowledge him, and he shall direct thy paths"
(Proverbs 3:6 KJV). Everything that we need is wrapped up in
God, he is our source. All we have to do is go to him and he
will lead us and guides us. There is not a manual on how to be a
mom; this is something that we learn along the way and from
our own mothers or mother figures that were in our lives. This
is another reason why we should go to God in prayer. It seems
that young ladies who are not that mature when they become a
mother (some of them) they tend to grow up. When I had my
first child it seemed like I really didn't try hard in life. But once
I had her I had a desire to go hard because of her.

I talk a lot about women and mothers in this book, which
there is nothing against the fathers. We have some good fathers
out there and together as women we need to support our men
and leaders. Women and mothers, you have the power to help
create leaders, fathers, and daughters. Life is hard that is why
we should tell our children the truth and teach them the right
paths to take in life. Always remember as a mother that it is
your job to protect your children and teach them the right way
of life. But as an adult if you are not sure the right way how can
you teach your children. Remember to find healing for yourself,
strive to do better in life, prepare for the future, and spend time
with your children. Every moment that you spend with them
will be a moment that they will care for the rest of their lives.
People talk about their childhood memories the ones that are
near and dear unto their hearts (or the one that is most
impactful to them) are usually the ones that they tell first. So,
what memories are you making with your children on a daily
basis? Are you pouring into the kids or are you taking away
from them? There are mothers out there who are not sure if
they are a good mother I just want you to know that no one is

perfect. Seek God first and do your best and you will be surprised the outcome of it all. God as entrusted you with the children you have. He already knew that you are capable of being good stewards over them and their lives.

# Chapter 11- Love (Agape)

Different people see love in different ways but in the new testament of the bible it talks a lot about a special kind of love. Most people refer to this love as an unconditional love, but it is actually a sacrificial love. The truth of the matter is there are different forms of love; you will not love your husband like you will love your children. The kind of love that Christ has loved us with is a selfless love, it's not a love full of self. When you truly love someone, you care about the needs of that person more than your own needs. The dictionary defines love as a profoundly tender, passionate affection for another person, or a feeling of warm personal attachment or deep affection, as for a parent, child, or friend. Now in the same dictionary **agape** love is defined as selfless love of one person for another without sexual implications (especially love that is spiritual in nature).

We need to see more of the agape type love in the church. A lot of Christian's talks about this love that Christ has loved us, but do we display it ourselves? Christ was an example of how we as Christians can live on this earth. There are people in this world who will never know Christ but what they see in you (Christians). If we don't show forth love are we showing forth Christ? Many times, we are so excited about how God loves us but then we throw stones at the next person, as if we live perfect lives. All the pain that we experience in life should not keep us from loving less. Loving more should be our agenda; Not just the love of finding a mate. But the love I speak about is the love that Christ removed himself from his throne to show us. Are you selfish? Do you think of yourself before you think of anyone else? Is that how Christ lived while he was on the earth and do we live like (how Christ lived) that now?

# He Was With Me All The Time

The bible actually speaks about real love and what it should display in 1 Corinthians chapter 13. In this passage, Paul speaks about how if he had all knowledge and gifts but has not love that he is nothing. This is the same with us if we go through life and fulfill every dream that we may have but have not love we have nothing. We need love in our lives and we need to show others love on a daily basis. When was the last time that you showed forth a selfless love? Love is also an action word; which Christ shows us every day of our being. Is love words that you just say or do you show forth love? When Christ walked this earth, he showed how much he loved us by healing the sick, raising the dead, and giving sight to the blind. Christ was all about restoring his people and making us whole. Have you truly showed someone that you loved them, by spending time with them;

If your children where asked a question of do your parents show you that they love you, could they say yes and actually tell someone how? Let's not allow pass negative situations rob us of true love, by building up walls to try and protect ourselves from being hurt by someone. Because honestly you are still being hurt but you are the one hurting yourself this time by building the invisible walls? The love that I am talking about is full of safety, compassion, and wholeness. The bible says that this kind of love will never fail and it will cover a multitude of sins (1 Peter 4:8), with love like this you will never lose. Even though there are different forms of love that we will experience in our life the agape is the one type of love that we should all mature in. There are people walking around filled with bitterness, anger, and hate and they are unleashing it on everyone that they come in contact with. But image a people

# He Was With Me All The Time

full of love that showed there love to all those around them. The truth is we as people have the power to impact this nation so how do you want to do it? Love yourself first is a way to impact this nation. There are so many people out there who do not love themselves, and there are so many of our children as well. I was once in a church service and the Pastor asked for people to come up who has ever struggled with rejection (all of their lives); almost the whole church went on stage. I stayed in my seat knowing that I should have ran to that alter and fell on the ground.

But I was so amazed at the number people who had struggled with the same problem that I had. Yet the whole time I felt that I was all alone and no one could understand my struggle. Then I was in another service and the minister asked for all those who have struggled with depression to come forth and there were so many kids and teenagers that it was mind blowing. Throughout this book I always say be honest with yourself and others. The reason why is because no one can help you if they don't know that you are hurting. The parents of all the kids had no idea that their child was struggling with that. I am glad that the kids were honest enough with themselves to stand up and inform someone of their hurts. Love you (people) and make yourself smile, you can spend time by yourself and enjoy it. There is no need to always have people around you to make yourself feel good about whom you are. What I find funny is that most women who suffer with hurt always find a guy that they are so in love with. Yet these women do not even love themselves so how can you love someone else. You will settle for anything when you haven't established a love for yourself. Have agape love for yourself. Love yourself unconditionally and through all you fault and struggles.

Then once you have done that you can successfully love someone else. Everyone on the planet and in this nation, deserves love and needs it. Sometimes you have to look at yourself in the mirror and say I do love myself even if you are exercising faith at that moment. Also, if we really think about it, why do people not love themselves? What could have possibly transpired in their life for them not to love themselves? As Christian the one thing that we should always show forth is love. God doesn't possess it but it is who God is. The next time someone asks you who is God really you respond by saying he is love. The agape love is a love that is spiritual and not sexual in its nature, so if you think about it our flesh can't ever love an agape type of love.

But our spirits can only love like this. The father of all spirits is love and if you have the father in you than you should have this same love. There is a surety that you have when you have this kind of love and that we all should have because father God loves us like this. One of the definitions for the word surety is "a pledge or formal promise made to secure against loss, damage, or default". The love that God has loved us with has placed a mark of surety on our lives and God has pledge to himself (because there is no power greater than him to pledge too) that he will love us through all that we go through. God will love us through pain, suffering, loss, death, and any damage that we acquire along the way. Who else can ever love you like that, but yourself? Once you have loved yourself like that then you can effectively love someone else including your children, husband, or friend. So, remember because God loves you like he do you can be sure of yourself and give others that same type of surety.

## He Was With Me All The Time

Love: Who can live without it because we all need it and we need it to function properly in our lives. Love hard, love more, love much, love every day, love each other, love when you hurt, love when your happy, love when you're up, love when your down, but most of all love yourself.

## Chapter 12 – What can God Do?

Out of all that I have went through in my life and believe me there is more than what I have talked about so far, I thank God for covering me. In the book of Revelations (Rev 3:20 KJV) it says "Behold, I **stand** at the **door**, and knock: if any man hears my voice, and opens the **door**, I will come in to him, and will sup with him, and he with me". This scripture has come to life in my life and it can come to life in yours as well. I allowed the Lord to come in to my heart and do surgery on it. My life has changed for the better and the Lord has truly been blessing me. I realize that through all that I have been through in life all the hurt, pain, and disappointments that God has been with me all the time.

I am sure that as you look at your life and go over things that you will realize that God has been with you as well. I am so grateful for a loving God because that is who he is. God is a good God and he protects us and covers us even when we are not thinking about him. To read the word of God and have it relate to my life is amazing. God can change you and he will if you allow him too. What I love most is that the change will come from the inside out. Most people try to change from the outside in, and that change is not effective. If you don't deal with something by the root, then the foundation is still there. The transformation that has taken place in my life is astonishing. To be in such a disgraceful state and then to experience healing like never before has change the way that I look at life. I mean it's like a fairy tale where I was the girl that became a princess and Jesus (my savior) is the king. This can be and is your life as well the only thing is you may not know that

66

it has already happen, like I didn't know. When you read the
bible, it talks about how Jesus didn't just heal people but he
made them whole. God wants us to be whole and not just
healed from whatever you may be suffering with. Life is so big
and yet for such a short time (no matter how old you live too)
most people do so few with their lives. We have a classification
of famous people in this world; truthfully, we all are famous
you just haven't tap into your talent yet. I think back on all the
sleepless nights and all the crying that I have done and my life
changed in the blink of an eye. I had come in contact with the
Spirit of the Living God. After being in his presence things
have changed about me that I can't even tell you when the
change took place. There are things that I stopped liking and
doing and I honestly can't tell you when I stop liking those
things.

God is real whither you choose to believe or not. He is waiting
on you to just let him in your heart so that he can show you
how real he is. My life was like a puzzle when it first comes out
the box it is in all these pieces and you have to put them in
order. Well I didn't even know what the picture was that I was
putting together. However, God knew and he took all my
pieces and he is placing them in order to bring forth a beautiful
picture. There is life after depression you are not the only one
out there hurting. Someone does care about you and you are
beautiful. You are great just the way you are and the size you
are. We are not all here to be the same or look the same, so be
yourself. Be the best (you) that you can be. I have seen this
video of this young boy who had a heart condition. He said
that he had died and was in this room and everything in the
room was white and it was filled with so much peace. While in
this place, the young man stated that when he looked back over

his life he was happy with the things that he has done. He was at peace with death. Can you say the same about your life? Your life is not all about you as funny as that sounds. It is more about the people that you will touch through your life. You don't' have to be a result of the cards that have been dealt to you. You can take those cards and make a brand-new card game out of them.

I always tell people don't let your problems stress you but you stress those problems. Help as many people as you can in life and be determined to live and be happy no matter what you see. How do you know you won't make it (in life) if you haven't even tried? Hang around people that will lift you up and tell you the truth. Teach your children how wonderful they are at young ages. Hold your head up high, square your shoulders back and live because you can. It is because we are different that each of us is special. Now what if we all were the same, then why would the other be special? Embrace who you are and your distinctions, trust God with your whole heart and fly.

You do have another enemy out there besides Satan and the name of that enemy is Average. Be extraordinary do wonderful things and make yourself proud. Don't worry about people. Because people will always have something to say about other people no matter what they do. But as long as you are happy that is all that matters. If you have dreams go after them hard and don't stop until you have reached all your goals. There are people who die every day but when will you make the choice to live? God has always been with you whither you believe it or not. The Creator has covered you from so much but he wants you to go higher and do more in life. You don't have to stay depressed, suicidal, or angry you can be happy. You can have the desires of your heart and be more than what you see. For the bible says that you are fearfully and wonderfully (Psalms 139:14 KJV) made. What shall we then say to these things? If God be for us, **who** can be **against** us (Romans 8:31 KJV)? Nothing can separate you from the love of Christ not even yourself. But you can choose not to embrace his love or be fulfilled in it. What will God do for you? EVERYTHING

# He Was With Me All The Time

He Was With Me All The Time

He Was With Me All The Time

He Was With Me All The Time

# He Was With Me All The Time

He Was With Me All The Time

www.ingramcontent.com/pod-product-compliance
Lightning Source LLC
Chambersburg PA
CBHW071238090426
42736CB00014B/3132